CONTENTS

INTRODUCTION

Once every four years, players and fans from all parts of the globe assemble in one country. There, they will watch the world's greatest footballers taking part in the biggest single sporting event – the FIFA World Cup.

Terrific Tournament

The FIFA World Cup is an international competition to find the best national football team in the world. Qualifying games occur in advance of each World Cup to determine which teams will attend; currently, 32 teams take part in the tournament, called the World Cup finals. Passions run incredibly high and, for players, the pressure mounts in the lead-up to the tournament. Ahead of the players is the ultimate test of their footballing ability and their coach's tactics. The pressure and intensity peaks for the two nations who contest the World Cup Final – the last game that will determine the world champions for the next four years. Winning the World Cup Final is the pinnacle of any footballer's career and is what top professional players dream of. For many smaller footballing nations, just playing in the tournament itself is their ultimate goal – a feat that over 70 nations, from Algeria to Zaire, have managed.

MAD /// /// FACT

In Sweden's match with England at the 2006 World Cup, Marcus Allback scored the World Cup's 2,000th goal.

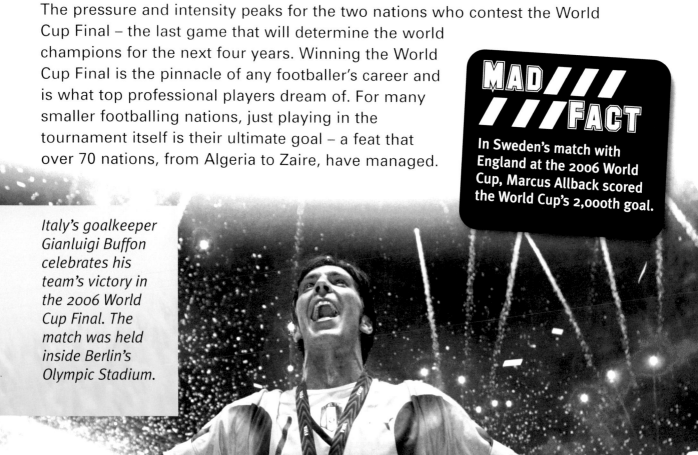

Italy's goalkeeper Gianluigi Buffon celebrates his team's victory in the 2006 World Cup Final. The match was held inside Berlin's Olympic Stadium.

Super Support

It is estimated that there are more than 240 million people around the world that regularly play organised football matches. For each of these players there are many more non-playing fans that support their national team, either by attending live matches or following avidly on television, radio, in newspapers and on the Internet. The 2006 tournament was filmed by hundreds of cameras and broadcast to television stations in 214 countries. More than 710 million people are believed to have watched the gripping 2006 Final between Italy and France.

Fans celebrate as Clint Mathis puts the US team ahead in a first round match at the 2002 World Cup.

Official Attendance at World Cups

Year	Total Attendance	Average per game
2006	3.36 million	52,491
2002	2.71 million	42,269
1998	2.79 million	43,517
1994	3.59 million	68,991
1990	2.52 million	48,411
1986	2.40 million	46,297
1982	2.11 million	35,698

Live Attendances

Since the very first World Cup in 1930, the competition has been held 18 times all over the world. Attendances have boomed and tickets are often snapped up years in advance.

In 1930, just over 300 people turned up to watch the first ever Final, played between Peru and Romania. However, 434,200 fans attended the other 17 games at a very healthy average of 25,541 spectators per match. At the 1994 World Cup, held in giant stadiums in the United States of America, more than 68,000 fans watched each game. When Brazil played Uruguay in the match to decide the winning team of the 1950 World Cup, 199,850 fans are estimated to have crammed into the newly-built Maracanã Stadium to watch.

MAD FACT

At the 1990 World Cup, the President of the United Arab Emirates promised a Rolls Royce to any player who scored for the UEA team. Two players scored and found new luxury cars waiting for them at home!

THEN AND NOW

Football developed in Britain in the nineteenth century before being exported around the world. By the 1920s, it was being played in dozens of countries and the demand for a worldwide football tournament was growing.

FIFA

The president of FIFA in the 1920s, Jules Rimet, campaigned hard for an international tournament. Football was already played at the Olympics, with Uruguay winning gold in both 1924 and 1928. As a result, when FIFA organised the first World Cup in 1930, Uruguay became the host.

> **MAD //// //// FACT**
>
> Hector Castro of the 1930 World Cup-winning team was missing his right hand. It was amputated in an accident when he was 13 years old.

The First World Cup

Only four teams from Europe – Belgium, France, Romania and Yugoslavia – made the two-week-long journey by ship to Uruguay, picking up the Brazilian team along the way. With home advantage and a very strict training regime, Uruguay become the first World Cup winners, defeating Argentina 4-2 in the Final. The match was refereed by Jean Langenus of Belgium, who wore golfing plus-four trousers, a jacket, tie and hat!

While most of the rules used today were already in place, there was no back pass rule and no substitutes. Although players could be sent off the field, referees were not equipped with red and yellow cards until 1970. The format of the tournament has also chopped and changed, with half the teams knocked out after one game in the 1934 World Cup and there being no one-match Final at the 1950 tournament.

Uruguay's Lorenzo Fernandez, Pedro Cea and Hector Scarone celebrate as their team wins the first ever World Cup Final in 1930.

The Trophy

The teams that reach the World Cup finals are playing for the most coveted trophy in world football. There have been two World Cup trophies – the first having a chequered history. Named the Jules Rimet Cup, it was won by Italy in 1934 and retained in 1938. During World War II, it was hidden under the bed of an Italian football official for fear of it being melted down. Stolen in London shortly before the 1966 World Cup, panic ensued until a dog found it in a garden. When Brazil won the World Cup for the third time in 1970, they were allowed to keep the trophy.

A new trophy made from five kilograms of solid gold, was commissioned and awarded to the 1974 winners. The original Jules Rimet trophy was stolen from Brazil in 1983 and has never been recovered. Winning teams today are given a gold-plated replica of the trophy.

MAD FACT

Uruguay and Argentina were so suspicious of one another in the 1930 Final that they both insisted on playing with their own football. In the end, each ball was used for a half.

Brazilian captain Cafu kisses the trophy after his side's victory in the 2002 World Cup. Each winning team's name is engraved on the trophy's base – there is enough space to list the winners until 2038.

⚽ WINNING THE BID

Once a national football organisation decides to enter into the bidding to host the World Cup, an organising committee prepares a bid. This has all the details of security, stadiums and transport links used for the tournament. This is presented to FIFA where the committee votes on which bid wins.

Bidding Nations

For some World Cups, such as those in 1954, 1958 and 1986, only one country made an official bid to host the tournament. Colombia was the only country to bid in 1986 but pulled out. When FIFA called for new bids, Mexico won and hosted the tournament for a second time. Apart from Mexico, and the USA in 1994, the first 16 World Cups were held either in Europe or South America. Since the boom in football in Asia and Africa, FIFA has awarded tournaments to these continents.

The 2010 World Cup

In 2002, the World Cup was co-hosted by Japan and South Korea. Since then FIFA has only accepted bids from one single country. As a result, a joint bid from Libya and Tunisia to host the tournament in 2010 had to be dropped. That left three bids from the African countries of Egypt, Morocco and South Africa. In May 2004, at FIFA's

A delighted Nelson Mandela poses with the World Cup trophy as he celebrates South Africa's successful bid to host the 2010 World Cup.

Who is...

...Franz Beckenbauer?

Germany's Franz Beckenbauer was a masterful footballer. He turned the defensive role of sweeper into a more attacking one, scoring 14 international goals in the process. He appeared at three World Cups, captaining West Germany to glory on home soil in 1974. Despite having little coaching experience, he was so popular in his home country that he was made West Germany's coach in 1984. In 1990, he became only the second man to win a World Cup as a player and as a coach. Beckenbauer campaigned for Germany's 2006 bid and became President of the Organising Committee for a tournament that was praised for its friendliness and for being very well organised.

headquarters in Zurich, Switzerland, it was announced that South Africa had won, making it the first African country to hold the tournament. Morocco, who had prepared bids for four of the five most recent World Cups, was once again disappointed.

Franz Beckenbauer speaks at a press conference during the 2006 World Cup. In three World Cups as a player, two as manager and one as leader of the Organising Committee, he never saw Germany or West Germany finish lower than third.

Uruguay never forgave the European nations for not playing in its 1930 World Cup. As a result, its team boycotted the 1934 tournament, making Uruguay the only champions never to defend the trophy.

Future World Cups

FIFA decided that the 2014 World Cup would be hosted in South America. There was just one bidding nation – Brazil – and its bid was approved in 2007. The scramble is already on for hosting World Cups after 2014. At least a dozen nations have already expressed an interest in hosting either the 2018 or 2022 tournament, including the USA, Russia, Indonesia and Japan. The winner of the 2018 bid will be announced in December 2010.

HOSTING THE WORLD CUP

The host nation can expect thousands of new visitors, either side of and during the tournament. Added to tourist facilities, the organisation needed to stage a World Cup successfully is enormous and very complex.

Football Facilities

Host nations have to spend millions in either upgrading old stadiums or building new ones in which World Cup matches will be played. While only three or four venues were needed in the past, the increased number of teams and matches in the tournament means that 10 or more stadiums are now used. A host nation has to provide secure accommodation and training facilities for the 32 teams, too. At the 2006 World Cup, more than 2,700 security staff were provided for the training camps and hotels. Transport also has to be laid on for the teams. At the 2006 tournament, the 32 teams travelled a staggering 64,000 kilometres, just from their base camp to the match stadiums.

MAD //// //// FACT

The 2006 World Cup's 'Fan Fest' events were a huge success, with 18 million attending and more than 3.5 million sausages sold!

The media gather at the 2006 World Cup game between Italy and USA. There were more than 14,000 journalists and other media staff present at the tournament.

More than Football

A host nation has to do far more than just provide football facilities. It has to organise ticketing, travel, transport and entertainment for fans. Extra medical staff, stewards and interpreters have to be trained while thousands of volunteers help make a visiting football fan's experience of the host country run smoothly. Ticketing can be an organisational nightmare – more than 15 million fans applied for the 3.34 million tickets to attend 2006 World Cup matches. For those without tickets, the organising committee developed 'Fan Fest' – events in German cities that provided 39 giant television screens for live football viewing as well as music, entertainment and food.

Media and Mascots

Journalists and television crews also flock to the host nation before and during the tournament. More than 18,000 members of the media attended the 2006 World Cup and the official 2006 website received 4,200 million hits during the tournament.

Since World Cup Willie in 1966, each World Cup has had its own mascot to help promote the tournament. The mascot is a major feature of the millions of pounds' worth of merchandise sold at each World Cup. The mascots have ranged from an orange, called Naranjito, in 1982 to a dog in 1994, a cockerel in 1998 and in 2006, a lion called Goleo.

Zakumi the leopard is the official mascot for the 2010 World Cup in South Africa.

REACHING THE FINALS

The first World Cup was by invitation only as 12 teams joined hosts, Uruguay. Since then, there have been qualifying matches to determine which nations will appear at the finals.

The Aim of Qualification

The many countries that want to take part in a World Cup tournament have to play a series of qualifying matches in the years between World Cups. A record 204 nations entered the qualifying stages for the 2010 competition. Each body, or confederation, that runs football in a region, organises its own qualifying. UEFA places its 53 European teams in groups with the winners guaranteed a place. CONMEBOL, which runs South American football, operates a league system with all of its ten nations playing each other twice.

Automatic Qualification

In 1934, Italy, despite being hosts of the tournament, still had to take part in qualifying. Since then, the host nation or nations win an automatic place. Until the 2006 tournament, the winner of the previous competition also did not have to qualify but Brazil for the 2006 tournament and Italy for the 2010 tournament have had to qualify.

Play-Offs

Each confederation is awarded a number of places at the finals. For the 2010 World Cup, Europe received 13 places, Africa 5 (plus the hosts, South Africa), South America 4.5, Asia

England's Theo Walcott looks for a way past a Croatian defender during a qualifer for the 2010 World Cup.

4.5, Oceania 0.5 and the CONCACAF region of North America, Central America and the Caribbean, 3.5 places. For the half places, teams in different regions compete in play-off games for a place at the tournament. For example, New Zealand, the winning Oceania team, plays the fifth placed African team for a place at the 2010 tournament.

Failure and Upsets

Only one nation has appeared at every single World Cup tournament – Brazil. Others have avoided entry, withdrawn in protest or failed to qualify. With so many teams competing for places, many major teams have lost out, especially in Europe. Russia failed to qualify in 2006 while the 1998 World Cup winners, France, failed to reach the finals in 1990 and 1994. Portugal is famous for its footballing superstars from Eusebio in the 1960s to Cristiano Ronaldo and Luis Figo, but astonishingly it has qualified for just four out of 18 World Cups. The Netherlands is also a renowned footballing nation yet it failed to qualify for six World Cups in a row before 1974 and was unsuccessful again in 2002.

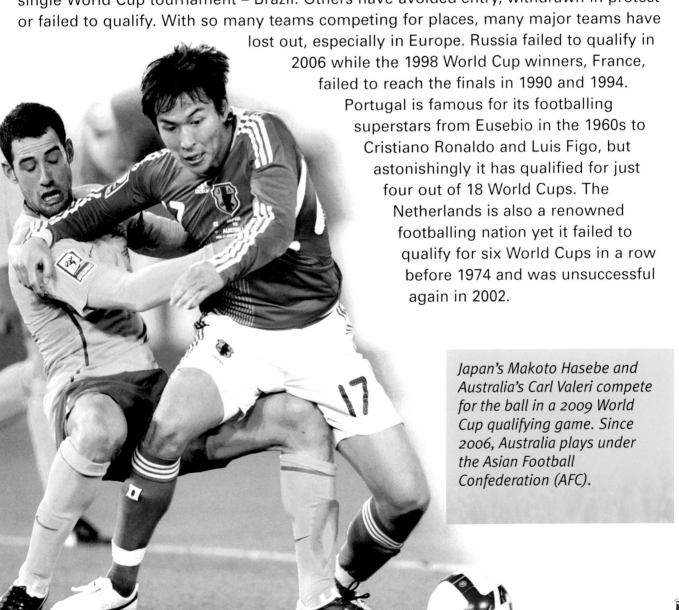

Japan's Makoto Hasebe and Australia's Carl Valeri compete for the ball in a 2009 World Cup qualifying game. Since 2006, Australia plays under the Asian Football Confederation (AFC).

COACHES

The pressure is on all players to perform at a World Cup but one person is under more pressure than any other. This is the manager or head coach of a World Cup team. Every decision he makes will be scrutinised by the world's media and fans.

Decisions, Decisions

At the 1930 World Cup, Romania's team was picked by its country's ruler, King Carol II. Today, coaches or managers head a large team of other coaches, medical experts and support staff who travel to the World Cup. Having selected his squad in advance (see page 18), a coach still has many decisions to make before each game. The precise make-up of his starting 11, what tactics he employs and when and how he uses his substitutes can have a major bearing on the outcome of each match. Against him are the world's best coaches who are managing rival sides. Perhaps, this is why only one coach has ever won the World Cup twice – Vittorio Pozzo, Italy's coach at the 1934 and 1938 World Cups.

MAD //// //// FACT

West Germany's coach, Helmut Schön, presided over 25 World Cup finals matches, from 1964 to 1978 – the most of any coach.

Substitutions and Criticisms

Up to three substitutes per game are allowed. These give a coach the chance to shake up his team, change tactics or to replace tired or injured players. Coaches expect criticism, even when it is unfair, if their team loses. However, some coaches have made major blunders. At the 1938 World Cup, for example, Brazilian coach Ademar Pimenta rested his star player, Leônidas, for the semi-final clash against Italy, which Brazil lost 2-1.

Foreign Coaches

No one has ever won the World Cup as coach of a foreign country's team. Brazilian Carlos Alberto Parreira, who won the World Cup with his home country in 1994, has also coached Kuwait, United Arab Emirates and Saudi Arabia to reach the finals. Arguably, the greatest achievement of a foreign coach was that of Guus Hiddink. South Korea had played in five tournaments without winning a game before he coached them to the semi-final of the 2002 World Cup.

Head coach of the French national team, Raymond Domenech, instructs his players during a training session before the 2006 World Cup Final.

SQUADS AND SEEDING

The squad selection, preparation and the team's seeding at the tournament are all crucial to how successful a team's World Cup journey will be.

Picking a Squad

The manager or coach has to select 23 players that will make up his squad. He must get the balance of his squad right, mixing experience with youth, making sure his squad offers a range of attacking threats and has enough cover for key players should they get injured. Managers and coaches often spring surprises when they select a squad. For example, the inclusion of 17-year-old Theo Walcott in the 2006 England squad was criticised, as was the exclusion of 17-year-old Diego Maradona from Argentina's 1978 World Cup squad. In the latter case, coach Cesar Luis Menotti's decision was justified when Argentina won the World Cup for the first time.

Brazilian players go through a work out before the start of the 2006 World Cup in Germany.

Preparation

Teams often play a series of warm-up or friendly games in the weeks before the World Cup. This allows the coach to assess form and fitness and may help him with team selection. A happy squad is crucial to success. Togo's 2006 World Cup preparation was anything but happy, with the players going on strike and the coach, Otto Pfister, resigning then re-taking the job just days before the team's opening match. Togo lost all three of its games.

South Africa's Lefa Tsutsulupa sprints past Chile's Marco Estrada during a friendly in 2009.

Seeding Teams

The seeding system is used to organise the group draw (see page 26). Teams are seeded 1–32 by a system that looks at performances at the previous two World Cups and the FIFA World Ranking. This is a measure of national teams' performance in all matches over the previous four years. Before 2006, the rankings were based on eight years of games. This led to criticisms that distant successes inflated teams' rankings for too many years.

Top Eight Seedings for the 2006 World Cup

Brazil	Mexico
England	France
Spain	Italy
Germany	Argentina

Losing Players

A coach can replace any seriously injured player in his squad up to 24 hours before the first game. Once that deadline has passed, he has to make do with the squad that remains. A coach can lose a number of players throughout a tournament to injuries or suspensions because of a red card or mounting yellow cards.

Sometimes, one injured player's misfortune is another's golden chance. There is no better example than Just Fontaine who only made the French squad for the 1958 World Cup because of another player's injury. He played as striker and scored a record 13 goals in the tournament.

SOLID DEFENCE

Few teams can hope to prosper at a World Cup without a sound, solid and skilful defence. Defenders have to be at their peak to deal with the cream of the world's strikers and midfielders. Goalkeepers have to marshal their team's defence and be alert to all threats to their goal.

Defensive Tactics

Teams may line up with three, four or five defenders. The precise way in which they are positioned and play can vary greatly. In the past, a team often played with a sweeper, a player positioned behind the main line of defenders who covered any opposition attacks. In the modern game, the sweeper is often replaced by a defensive midfielder with the full backs, the two defenders nearest the sidelines, being really mobile and joining in the attack. Full backs such as Germany's Philipp Lahm and France's Patrice Evra are known for their linking play in attack, while Brazil's Roberto Carlos, a wingback, took some of the most powerful shots in football. Tall central defenders also pose a goal threat at corners and free kicks. The very last goal to be scored at the 2006 World Cup, for example, was a header by the Italian defender Marco Materazzi.

Ruud van Nistelrooy is tackled by Serbia and Montenegro's Goran Gavrančić. Gavrančić was part of his team's strong defence, which let in only one goal during the qualifying stages for the 2006 World Cup.

Great Goalkeepers

The World Cup has seen some outstanding performances from goalkeepers. These include legendary keepers such as Lev Yashin, Gordon Banks, Dino Zoff (see page 43) and Spain's Ricardo Zamora who, in 1934, became the first keeper to save a penalty at a World Cup. Goalkeepers and defenders pride themselves on keeping clean sheets – not conceding a goal during a game. Walter Zenga was in goal when Italy established a World Cup record at the 1990 tournament. He and his team had not let in a goal in 517 minutes of finals action. England's Peter Shilton appeared at three World Cups and managed ten clean sheets in total. His record tally was tied by France's Fabien Barthez in 2006. However, not losing games does not guarantee advancement. The Swiss team and its keeper, Pascal Zuberbühler, did not let in a single goal during the entire 2006 World Cup. However, the team lost in a penalty shootout to Ukraine in the Round of 16.

Who is...

...Gianluigi Buffon?

Gianluigi Buffon has made more than 90 appearances for Italy, his national team. In 2001, he became the world's most expensive goalkeeper when he was transferred from Parma to Juventus for about £32 million. Unflappable, confident and a brave shot-stopper, he conceded only two goals in the 2006 World Cup finals, one of which was a team-mate's own goal, the other, a penalty in the Final. Given this excellent record, it was no surprise when he was named goalkeeper of the competition.

Gianluigi Buffon dives to collect the ball near his post. His concentration and timing has made him one of the world's best goalkeepers.

⚽ MIDFIELD MAESTROS

Most teams line up with four or five midfielders in their side. These players need to be terrifically fit as they have to cover large amounts of ground in helping their side both defend and attack. A typical midfielder covers more than 12 km in the 90 minutes of a match.

Midfield Tactics

Different teams play different numbers and combinations of midfielders. Many teams play one or two wingers, players with great ball skills such as Cristiano Ronaldo and Frank Ribery. Other teams play with a more compact midfield. In the most recent World Cups, many teams have found success playing an anchor man, or defensive midfielder, just in front of the defence. This player breaks up opposition attacks and helps protect his defence. Ghana's Michael Essien, Italy's Gennaro Gattuso and France's Patrick Viera are amongst the most heralded in the anchor man position.

Pass Masters

World Cup midfielders are expected to be superb passers of the ball, able to hit simple balls to keep possession or strike a long pass or through ball to release a team-mate in a goalscoring position. Playmakers, such as Argentina's Lionel Messi, Italy's Andrea Pirlo and Spain's Xavi, are midfielders around which a side builds its attacks. They can help control the tempo or speed of a team's play by choosing to probe patiently or go for long passes and quick breaks.

Argentinian midfielder Lionel Messi moves away from Brazil's Luis Fabiano during a World Cup qualifying match.

Who is...

...Zinédine Zidane?

For much of the late 1990s and early 2000s, Zinédine Zidane was the best midfielder in the world. Possessing an incredible eye for a pass or goalscoring chance and sublime ball-control skills, Zidane became the world's most expensive footballer in 2001. He was transferred from Juventus, who had paid £3 million for him in 1996, to Real Madrid for more than £46 million. Zidane starred at the 1998 World Cup, scoring two goals in the Final as France beat Brazil. After winning Euro 2000, a thigh injury kept him out of two of France's three 2002 World Cup games. He came out of international retirement in 2005 to record his 100th appearance for France and was his team's captain during their 2006 World Cup campaign. Whilst he was sent-off in the Final, his penalty earlier in the game made him one of only four players (with Pelé, Paul Breitner and Vava) to score in two World Cup Final matches. He was voted the player of the 2006 tournament.

Goals from Midfield

As strikers are closely marked by opposition defenders, midfielders with great skill or explosive shots are often important goalscorers. The Brazilian Jairzinho possessed not only a powerful shot but also the ability to bend the ball skilfully through the air. At the 1970 World Cup, he scored in every match on his way to recording a career total of 33 goals for Brazil. Robert Prosinecki is the only man to score for two different countries at World Cup tournaments – for Yugoslavia in 1990 and for Croatia in 1998.

Two great midfield playmakers, Andrea Pirlo (left) and Zinédine Zidane compete for the ball in the 2006 World Cup Final.

GOAL!

Goals always win games and in the World Cup a single goal can make a massive difference. Since France's Lucien Laurent scored the first World Cup goal against Mexico in 1930, there have been more than 2,000 goals scored at World Cup finals.

Scoring Goals

Strikers are on the pitch to make or score goals. Only one of the 12 leading World Cup goalscorers (Teófilo Cubillas, see page 25) was not a striker. Goals can range from short-range tap-ins or blasts from distance to shots at the end of a long, free-flowing move. Argentina's second goal in their 6–0 thrashing of Serbia and Montenegro at the 2006 World Cup was a close-range shot from Ernesto Cambiasso following an amazing 24 passes in a row. In contrast, German striker, Miroslav Klose's five goals at the 2002 World Cup were all headers. Klose scored a further five goals at the 2006 tournament. The only other player to do this was Peru's Teófilo Cubillas whose 10 goals are the most scored by any midfielder.

see page 25

MAD /// FACT

Oleg Salenko's six World Cup goals for Russia included five scored in one game against Cameroon at the 1994 World Cup. In the Cameroon team was Roger Milla, the World Cup's oldest goalscorer at 42.

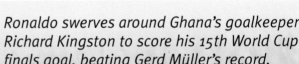
Ronaldo swerves around Ghana's goalkeeper Richard Kingston to score his 15th World Cup finals goal, beating Gerd Müller's record.

Hat-Tricks

The 2006 World Cup was the only one in which no player scored a hat-trick. Some 48 hat-tricks have been recorded but only four players (Sándor Kocsis, Gerd Müller, Just Fontaine and Gabriel Batistuta) have scored hat-tricks in two World Cup games. A hat-trick on a player's international debut, which just happens to be at a World Cup, is a feat players can only dream about, but Guillermo Stábile of Argentina managed this in 1930. The quickest hat-trick was netted by László Kiss for Hungary against El Salvador in 1982. The striker took just seven minutes to score the three goals.

S T A T   A T T A C K

Most World Cup Finals Goals

15 Ronaldo 1998, 2002, 2006

14 Gerd Müller 1970, 1974

13 Just Fontaine 1958

12 Pelé, 1958, 1962, 1966, 1970

11 Sándor Kocsis 1954

11 Jürgen Klinsmann 1990, 1994, 1998

10 Miroslav Klose 2002, 2006

10 Helmut Rahn 1954, 1958

10 Teófilo Cubillas 1970, 1978

10 Grzegorz Lato 1974, 1982

10 Gary Lineker 1986, 1990

10 Gabriel Batistuta 1994, 1998, 2002

Who is...

...Ronaldo?

Sometimes criticised for his movement and fitness, no one doubts that Brazil's Ronaldo is one of football's most lethal strikers. A natural eye for goal and quick acceleration have helped Ronaldo to outfox many of the world's best defenders. He has played for various clubs, including Cruzeiro where he started his career, and Real Madrid who paid over £28 million for his services in 2002, a short time after he had starred at the World Cup and been its leading goalscorer. At the 2006 tournament, with two goals against Japan and one against Ghana, he became the World Cup's all-time leading goalscorer.

THE GROUP STAGES

The first matches in the World Cup finals are in the group stages. This is where teams play all the other members of their group in order to qualify to play in the first knockout round. After they have qualified, the top two teams from each group play in the Round of 16.

World Cup Draw

The World Cup draw is made a number of months before the tournament begins. The draw puts teams into eight groups, labelled A to H, each containing four teams for the group stages of the tournament. Teams are placed in pots according to their seeding (see page 19). At the 2006 World Cup, the top eight seeds were all placed in the same pot so that only one top-eight team would be placed in any group. Other teams were placed in pots by region so that maximum of two European sides and only one from any other region were placed in a single group.

MAD //// //// FACT

At the 1954 World Cup, West Germany suffered an 8-3 defeat by Hungary in the group stage. The two teams met in the final with West Germany triumphing 3-2.

Groups of Death

The aim of the draw is to create fair and competitive groups. However, the media pick up on the tough groups and label them the 'Groups of Death'. At the 1958 World Cup, the Group of Death featured Argentina, a top-rated Czechoslovakian side, world champions West Germany, and Northern Ireland, the smallest country to qualify for the Finals. Astonishingly, Northern Ireland made it to the next stage at the expense of West Germany.

Group B (draw board)

1 ENGLAND
2 PARAGUAY
3 TRINIDAD & TOBAGO
4 SWEDEN

Group B is displayed during the group draw for the 2006 World Cup. Many England fans were relieved at the draw, which was one of the easier World Cup groups.

Spain's striker Raul shows quick reactions to get in between Tunisia's defender and goalkeeper to score during a 2006 Group H game.

Group Upsets

The 2002 World Cup was one full of surprises. Its opening game definitely set the tone, with a victory by Senegal over the then world champions, France. Senegal and Denmark qualified from Group A at the expense of France and Uruguay. Defeat in the first game does not necessarily mean that a team's chances of surviving the group stage are over. At the 1994 World Cup, Saudi Arabia lost their first match but won their next two to progress. In 1982, Italy drew all three of their group games. However, the team just nudged ahead of Cameroon in its group because it had scored one more goal. The Italians then went on to win the competition. While all of the top eight seeded teams progressed from their group at the 2006 World Cup, there were still upsets. Australia qualified from Group F at the expense of Croatia and Japan, while Switzerland topped Group G ahead of France, South Korea and Togo.

MAD FACT

At the 1986 World Cup Group D game between Uruguay and Scotland, Uruguay's José Alberto Batista received a red card in just 56 seconds – a new World Cup record.

IT'S A KNOCKOUT

After the group stages, teams enter the knockout stages. This is win or lose time, with single games to determine who goes through to the next knockout round.

Round of 16

Eight knockout games make up the Round of 16, with the winning teams reaching the quarter-finals. The winners of each group play the runners-up in another group. As the basic draw is known in advance, some teams really push to win their group knowing that they will avoid a top-ranked team in this round. For example, at the 2006 World Cup, England managed to top Group B ahead of Sweden. This gave them an easier match against Group A's runners-up (Ecuador) while Sweden had to play Group A's winners, the formidable Germany.

Steven Gerrard leaps high to head the ball away from Ecuador's Giovanny Espinoza during a Round of 16 game at the 2006 World Cup. A trademark free kick from David Beckham gave England a narrow 1-0 victory over the South American side.

Who is...

...Diego Maradona?

Argentina's Diego Maradona is one of the most talented and controversial footballers to appear at a World Cup. He made his debut for his country in 1982, and was the undoubted star of the 1986 tournament. He scored a controversial goal against England when he punched the ball into the net with his hand. He followed this by scoring again after an amazing run from inside his own half past six England players. This second goal was voted FIFA's Goal of the Century. A similar goal helped Argentina beat Belgium and go on to win the tournament. Although Maradona did not have the same impact at the 1990 World Cup, Argentina were still runners-up. At the 1994 competition, Maradona was sent home after failing a drugs test. In November 2008, he was appointed coach of Argentina's national team.

Quarter- and Semi-Finals

Eight teams make the quarter-finals, knowing just two more victories will take them to a World Cup Final. Matches at the quarter- and semi-final stage are often cagey affairs with the emphasis on defence. For example, three of the four 1986 quarter-finals ended in draws and were decided by penalties. Exceptions include Croatia's shock demolition of Germany 3-0 at the 1998 World Cup and before that, an astonishing 1954 quarter-final in which Switzerland went three goals up in just 19 minutes only for Austria to score five goals, all before half time. The end result was 7-5 – the most goals ever scored in a World Cup finals game.

Diego Maradona parades the World Cup trophy after powering Argentina to victory in the 1986 competition.

SHOOTOUTS

In the knockout stages of the World Cup, if the scores are level after 90 minutes and after extra time, a penalty shootout is used to decide the outcome of the match.

Deciding Draws

During a shootout the teams stand in the centre circle with only the penalty taker and goalkeeper close to the goal. The referee picks the end from which all the penalties are taken and a coin toss determines which team goes first. Teams take alternate penalties, five each, to determine a winner. If the scores are level after five penalties each, the shootout enters its 'sudden death' phase. Two penalties are taken, one each by a player from each team, until one player scores and the other misses.

A Test of Nerve

After 120 minutes of top-class football, with their lungs bursting and legs aching, players have to step up and take penalties. Teams decide the order in which players take penalties before the shootout begins. Coaches may have worked on this in advance during training but many look at and talk to players in the minutes before a shootout to determine who they think is in the best frame of mind. According to a 2006 study, just over two-thirds of penalties in a shootout are scored despite the overwhelming advantage to the penalty taker. The penalties that fail are sometimes bad misses, but may be due to the goalkeeper's skill, such as when Iker Casillas saved two Republic of Ireland penalties to help Spain reach the 2002 quarter-finals.

US goalkeeper Briana Scurry saves a penalty from China's Liu Ying at the 1999 Women's World Cup.

Golden Goals

FIFA experimented with other options after full time, including the 'golden goal'. This meant that the team that scored the first goal in extra time won. The golden goal rule was used in all FIFA competitions, including the World Cup, from 1993 to 2004. France's game against Paraguay in the 1998 tournament was the first game to be decided by golden goal, while at the next World Cup, Senegal beat Sweden but lost to Turkey in the quarter-final with both games decided by a golden goal.

France's Thierry Henry lies dejected after his team loses the 2006 World Cup Final shootout against Italy.

STAT ATTACK

Shootouts in recent finals

Year	Match	Result	Penalties
1998	Argentina v England	2-2	4-3
1998	France v Italy	0-0	4-3
1998	Brazil v Netherlands	1-1	4-2
2002	Spain v Rep. Ireland	1-1	3-2
2002	South Korea v Spain	0-0	5-3
2006	Ukraine v Switzerland	0-0	3-0
2006	Germany v Argentina	1-1	4-2
2006	Portugal v England	0-0	3-1
2006	Italy v France	1-1	5-3

Winners and Losers

West Germany and Germany have never lost a World Cup shootout in four attempts. However, England have been knocked out of three World Cups (1990, 1998, 2006) by losing penalty shootouts. The first World Cup Final to be decided by a penalty shootout was in 1994. Roberto Baggio of Italy sent the ball high over the crossbar to hand victory to Brazil. In 2006. Italian football fans were happier when Italy beat France 5-3 in a shootout to become champions.

As the tournament draws to its climax, there are several awards to be won, apart from the winning team's trophy. These include individual awards to star players, the selection of the team of the tournament and the play-off game for third place.

MAD //// //// FACT

During the 2002 World Cup, Turkey's Hakan Şükür scored the World Cup's fastest ever goal in just 11 seconds as his team beat South Korea 3-2 in the third place play-off.

Golden Shoe and Ball

The tournament's leading goalscorer receives the Golden Shoe award. This prize may be shared by a number of goalscorers. In 1958, the award went to France's Just Fontaine who scored 13 goals in just six games. In 2006, it was won by Germany's Miroslav Klose, who scored five goals.

Since 1982, a Golden Ball has also been awarded to the World Cup's best player. A committee of coaches and ex-players studies the matches and, after the semi-finals, draws up a shortlist of ten players. These are then voted for by media representatives. Scoring goals or being a member of the World Cup winning team is no guarantee of scooping this award. It went to a goalkeeper in 2002 and a midfielder in 2006. Both were on the losing side in the Final.

STAT ATTACK

Golden Ball Winners

1982 Paolo Rossi

1986 Diego Maradona

1990 Salvatore Schillaci

1994 Romário

1998 Ronaldo

2002 Oliver Kahn

2006 Zinédine Zidane

Oliver Kahn saves the ball during the 2002 World Cup. The German keeper helped Germany obtain five clean sheets as they reached the Final.

Other Tournament Awards

An All-Star team is selected from all the players at the finals. Originally, it was just 11 players but today, a 23-man squad is selected. The 2002 All-Star team was the first to contain players from Senegal, Turkey and South Korea. Franz Beckenbauer is the only player to be named in three separate All-Star teams (1966, 1970 and 1974). At the 2006 World Cup, Germany's Lukas Poldolski won a new award for the Best Young Player of the tournament. Players of 21 years or under are eligible for the trophy. The Lev Yashin award, named after the legendary Soviet Union goalkeeper, goes to the best goalkeeper. A public Internet vote is held for the most entertaining team of the tournament. Brazil in 1994 and France in 1998 were predictable winners, South Korea's surprising run to the semi-finals won them the award in 2002.

MAD FACT

Seven of the 11 1930 All-Star team were from Uruguay. An eighth was US player, Bert Patenaude, who in 2006 was officially awarded the status of the first World Cup hat-trick scorer by FIFA.

Third Place Play-Off

A match between the beaten semi-finalists for third place first took place in 1934 between Germany and Austria. After happening again in 1938, it has been a regular feature only since 1958. Players and coaches have to fight their disappointment at failing to reach the Final to prepare for the third-place contest. Germany did so successfully before their own fans in the 2006 play-off game in which they beat Portugal 3-1.

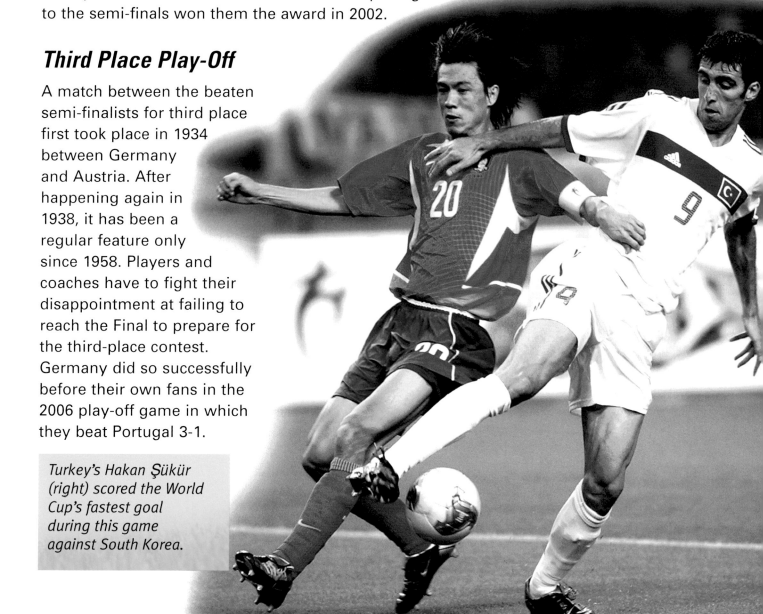

Turkey's Hakan Şükür (right) scored the World Cup's fastest goal during this game against South Korea.

WORLD CUP CHAMPIONS

While more than 200 have tried, the football teams of only 11 nations have ever reached a World Cup Final. They are just a single game away from the ultimate in football glory – lifting the World Cup trophy as world champions.

The Final

The World Cup Final is run in the same way as any football match, but everyone knows, especially the players, that it is the biggest match in world football. Players entering a Final do so with a mixture of pride at coming so far and nerves. No player wants to be the one who makes a critical mistake or ends up on the losing side. Four nations have never won the World Cup but have been runners-up: the Netherlands, Czechoslovakia, Sweden and Hungary. One player, Karl-Heinz Rummenigge of West Germany, has captained two losing teams in World Cup Finals in 1982 and 1986.

STAT ATTACK

Winners and Runners-Up

Date	Winners	Runners-Up
1930	Uruguay	Argentina
1934	Italy	Czechoslovakia
1938	Italy	Hungary
1950	Uruguay	Brazil
1954	West Germany	Hungary
1958	Brazil	Sweden
1962	Brazil	Czechoslovakia
1966	England	Germany
1970	Brazil	Italy
1974	West Germany	Netherlands
1978	Argentina	Netherlands
1982	Italy	West Germany
1986	Argentina	West Germany
1990	West Germany	Argentina
1994	Brazil	Italy
1998	France	Brazil
2002	Germany	Brazil
2006	Italy	France

Italian captain Fabio Cannavaro holds the trophy aloft as Italy celebrate their 2006 win.

?

Who is...

...Pelé?

Pelé is considered by many to be the greatest ever footballer and is the only player to have been part of three World Cup winning squads. He debuted for leading Brazilian club Santos when he was 15 years old and earned the first of 91 caps for his national team at 16. A year later, at the 1958 World Cup, his hat-trick in the semi-final and two goals in the Final made him famous. Pelé scored a record 77 goals for Brazil and was known for his incredible vision and ball skills. He was also a courageous and sporting player who gained fans wherever he played. After a major part in Brazil's 1970 World Cup campaign, he retired from international football a year later. An estimated 180,000 fans packed into the Maracanã stadium in Brazil to see his last game.

World Cup Winners

Having won five times, Brazil is the most successful World Cup country. The team's first win was in 1958 and its last in 2002 after being runners-up to France in 1998. Brazil is also the only nation to have won World Cups away from South America: in Sweden in 1958, Mexico in 1970 and in South Korea and Japan in 2002. Italy has won four times and became the first nation to win back-to-back World Cups with their victories in 1934 and 1938. Italy's first triumph was as hosts and, since that time, five host nations have won the World Cup.

The brilliant Pelé in action at the 1966 World Cup, weaving his way past the Bulgarian defence. Pelé scored, but was later injured in this match.

SHOCKS AND SURPRISES

All eyes are on the players in the most favoured teams at a World Cup, but drama, shocks and surprises occur throughout each tournament.

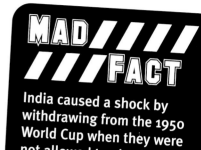

MAD FACT

India caused a shock by withdrawing from the 1950 World Cup when they were not allowed to play barefoot!

Giant Killers

The footballing giants of Europe and South America have fallen to lesser-rated sides on many occasions. One of the most famous was at the 1950 World Cup, where the England team of professional footballers was beaten 1-0 by a United States team whose goalscorer, Joseph Gaetjens, washed dishes for a living. Italy was knocked out of the 1966 tournament by North Korea and by South Korea at the 2002 World Cup. South Korea added Portugal and Spain to their scalps as they reached the semi-finals. World Cup hosts have not been immune to shocks, the biggest being West Germany's 2-1 defeat at the hands of Algeria in 1982.

Italy's Marco Materazzi falls after Zinédine Zidane headbutts him in the chest. Zidane was sent off for this during the 2006 Final.

Controversy and Tragedy

What followed West Germany's loss to Algeria was more shocking: West Germany beat Austria 1-0 in a largely attack-free game, allowing both countries to qualify from their group at the expense of Algeria. A 1989 World Cup qualifier game between Brazil and Chile ended in farce as the Chilean goalkeeper pretended that he had been injured by a missile thrown by a member of the crowd. Most shocking of all was the tragedy that befell the Zambian national team in 1993. On the way to a World Cup qualifier against Senegal, the team's aeroplane crashed, killing 18 players.

Refereeing Shocks

Sometimes, it is not the players who cause the upsets and drama, but the officials. At the 1982 World Cup, referee Miroslav Stupar changed his decision and disallowed a French goal after the head of the Kuwait Football Association, Prince Fahid, came onto the pitch and argued with him. Regardless of the disallowed goal, France still beat Kuwait 4-1. At the 2006 World Cup, Russian referee Valentin Ivanov officiated a particularly difficult game between Portugal and the Netherlands. By the end of the game, he had sent off four players and shown 16 yellow cards – a World Cup record. In the Australia versus Croatia match at the same tournament, English referee Graham Poll caused a stir by showing Josip Simuniç two yellow cards without sending him off. Simuniç then received a third yellow card from Poll at the end of the game! As a result, Poll was sent home.

Ahn Jung-Hwan throws his boots into the crowd after South Korea recorded one of the biggest upsets in World Cup history, beating Italy 2–1 after extra time in 2002.

MAD FACT

Ahn Jung-Hwan was playing on loan for Italian club AC Perugia at the time his goal knocked Italy out of the World Cup. Perugia's chairman Luciano Gaucci cancelled the South Korean's contract.

THE WOMEN'S WORLD CUP

After much lobbying by women's football associations, the first Women's World Cup tournament was held in China in 1991. Since that time there have been some brilliant performances and dramatic moments.

Early Tournaments

In 1991 a total of 12 teams were invited to attend the first Women's World Cup finals. The team from the United States won all its games and the tournament, beating Norway in the Final. Propelled by star players such as Mia Hamm and Michelle Akers, the United States went on to build a strong record in subsequent tournaments, never finishing lower than third and winning the tournament twice. Norway continued its good form at the 1995 tournament, held in the neighbouring country of Sweden. The Norwegian team scored 17 goals in its three games during the group stage, knocked out the United States in the semi-finals and then went on to beat Germany 2-0 in the Final.

Brazil beat New Zealand 5–0 during their 2007 World Cup game – Marta (right) went on to be the tournament's leading scorer that year with seven goals.

Reaching the Finals

Qualification has developed since the first tournament. For the 2007 Women's World Cup, Europe was granted five places, South America and Africa two places and Oceania one place. North and Central America were granted 2.5 places and Asia 3.5. This meant that a team from each region had to contend play-off games to reach the final. In the two-match play-off, Japan narrowly beat Mexico to keep up its record of appearing at every World Cup final. Seven other nations have also managed that feat – Germany, USA, Sweden, China, Norway, Brazil and Nigeria. Unlike the men's World Cup, qualification in the different regions is usually by finishing in a high place in an organised competition. For the 2007 tournament, the United States and Canada qualified by reaching the final of the 2006 Women's Gold Cup – the continental competition for national teams from North and Central America.

Women's World Cup winners

1991 United States
1995 Norway
1999 United States
2003 Germany
2007 Germany

The 1999 World Cup

The 1999 Women's World Cup was held in the United States and was the first to feature 16 teams. There were goals aplenty with both Brazil beating Mexico and the United States beating Nigeria 7-1. The Final between China and the United States was watched by 90,185 spectators, the biggest ever attendance at a women's sports event. The Final was an epic yet goalless tussle, ending in a dramatic penalty shootout in which Briana Scurry, the United States' goalkeeper, saved Liu Ying's penalty.
The third place play-off between Brazil and Norway also went to penalties, with Brazil winning 5-4.

Mia Hamm celebrates after scoring the first goal of the 1999 World Cup in the United States' opening match against Denmark.

Into the Twenty-First Century

The United States became the first nation to host the tournament twice when in 2003, a SARS epidemic meant that China could not run the tournament. Germany scored 25 goals in the 2003 tournament and their ability told as they beat Sweden 2-1 in the Final with a golden goal. The Germans were even more dominant in the 2007 competition held in China. They did not concede a single goal in their seven matches. Throughout the tournament's 32 matches, 111 goals were scored. For the first time ever, teams received prize money with Germany as champions winning US$1 million.

Who is...

...Birgit Prinz?

Prinz is an athletic striker, great in the air, and has a fabulous eye for goal. She has scored more than 100 times for Germany in international games and was voted Germany's best female player for eight seasons in a row. At the 2003 World Cup, Prinz scored seven goals to finish the tournament as the leading scorer and was also awarded the Golden Ball as the tournament's best player. She followed this with a further five goals at the 2007 World Cup to make her the leading goalscorer with a total of 14 goals.

Birgit Prinz controls a high ball under pressure from Japanese defender Hiromi Isozaki.

MAD FACT

In a qualifying game for the 2003 tournament, a match between Trinidad and Tobago and Surinam was abandoned when Surinam had three players sent off and went down to six players when two others were injured.

Sweden's goalkeeper Caroline Joensson dives to save a goal during the 2003 World Cup Final match against Germany. The game went into extra time and was finally decided by a goal from Germany's Nia Kuenzer.

STAT ATTACK

Women's World Cup Golden Shoe Winners

1991 Michelle Akers (USA)
10 goals

1995 Ann-Kristen Aarønes (Norway) 6 goals

1999 Sissi (Brazil)
7 goals

Sun Wen (China)
7 goals

2003 Birgit Prinz (Germany)
7 goals

2007 Marta (Brazil)
7 goals

The 2011 Tournament

Germany held off interest from Australia, France, Canada, Switzerland and Peru to host the tournament in 2011. The women's game is very popular in Germany, and 23 German cities applied to host matches; these were whittled down to just nine cities. The opening match and Final will be played in the Olympic Stadium in Berlin, which can hold 74,000 spectators. Germany qualify automatically as hosts, while 15 other nations will gain places through qualifying games. In Europe, there are up to five places at the finals available for the 41 European teams competing in eight groups. England's group, for example, contains Austria, Spain, Turkey and Malta.

WORLD CUP LEGENDS

Many great footballers, from George Best and Ryan Giggs to George Weah and Alfredo Di Stefano, have never appeared at a World Cup finals, but many more have graced the tournament. Here are five true World Cup legends.

Johann Cruyff

The most gifted European player of his generation, Cruyff played with amazing vision and skill in a Dutch team that reached the Final of the 1974 World Cup only to be defeated by Germany. Cruyff was a versatile player and a lethal goalscorer, with an excellent strike rate of 33 goals in just 48 games. He refused to go to the 1978 World Cup out of concern for his family after a kidnap attempt and because of the political situation in the host country, Argentina.

Manuel Francisco dos Santos

One of the most entertaining players, dos Santos was nicknamed *Garrincha*, meaning 'little bird', because he was small. Although one of his legs was six centimetres shorter than the other, he was a mesmerising winger with incredible dribbling and ball skills. He won the World Cup with Brazil in 1958 and 1962. In 1962 he was voted player of the tournament.

Johann Cruyff leaves the Argentinian goalkeeper on the floor as he scores his first of two goals in a 1974 game.

Bobby Charlton

Bobby Charlton was part of the England squad for the 1958 World Cup but came to prominence in the 1962 and 1966 tournaments. With his brother Jack in central defence, Charlton played as an attacking midfielder in the England team that won the 1966 World Cup. Packing a fearsome shot, he also appeared at the 1970 tournament

Gerd Müller

Müller was short and squat but had a superb eye for goal. He was a prolific goalscorer for his club, Bayern Munich, and his country, netting 68 goals in just 62 appearances. Müller had a sensational 1970 World Cup, scoring two hat-tricks against Bulgaria and Peru and two goals in West Germany's 4-3 loss to Italy. He added further goals in the 1974 tournament, including the crucial winning goal which made West Germany champions for the first time since 1954.

Müller (left) scores the decisive goal in the 1974 World Cup Final.

Dino Zoff

A sensational goalkeeper, Dino Zoff made his international debut for Italy in 1968 and was part of Italy's winning European Championship team. Known for his intense levels of concentration and great shot stopping skill, Zoff played for Italy a record 112 times and featured in 17 World Cup finals games, losing only three. Zoff led Italy into the 1982 World Cup as captain and broke records to become the oldest player to win the World Cup.

Dino Zoff prepares to throw the ball out at the 1982 World Cup. Zoff's calm presence in goal was a major factor in Italy's World Cup victory.

 # GLOSSARY

AFC Short for the Asian Football Confederation, the organisation responsible for running football in Asia.

Clean sheet When a team manages to complete a game without conceding a goal.

CONCACAF Short for the *Confederación Norte-Centroamericana y del Caribe de Fútbol*, the regional organisation that runs football in North and Central America and the Caribbean.

CONMEBOL Short for the *Confederación Sudamericana de Fútbol*, the body that runs football in South America.

Disallowed goal A goal that is scored but does not count because the referee or his assistants spot a foul or an infringement.

Extra time A way of deciding a match in the event of a draw. Extra time involves two equal-length periods of additional play.

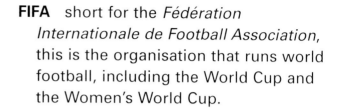

FIFA short for the *Fédération Internationale de Football Association*, this is the organisation that runs world football, including the World Cup and the Women's World Cup.

Golden goal A system used in extra time where the first goal to be scored wins the game for the scoring team.

Hat-trick When a player scores three goals in a single football match.

Knock-out round Any round of the World Cup in which the losing team is out of the tournament and the winning team progresses to the next round.

Marked When an attacking player is guarded closely to prevent him or her from receiving the ball.

Mascot A character used to promote a particular World Cup tournament.

Merchandise Souvenirs, clothing and other items for sale, bought by fans.

OFC Short for Oceania Football Confederation, the body that runs football in Oceania.

Penalty shootout A method of deciding a drawn game by a series of penalties all taken at one end of the pitch.

Play-off A match, pair or series of matches used to decide a final.

Professionals   Players who are paid to play football.

Red card   A card shown by the referee to send a player off the field. The sent-off player cannot be replaced so the team continues with one less player.

Runners-up   The team that finishes second.

SARS   Short for Severe Acute Respiratory Syndrome, this is a disease caused by a virus that spread in Asia from 2002.

Seeding   A way of ranking the teams at a World Cup so that the draw for the groups includes teams of differing abilities.

Substitutions   The way a team's line-up is changed by replacing one player on the pitch with another from the substitutes' bench.

Sweeper   A defender that plays closest to his or her own goal behind the rest of the defenders.

UEFA   Short for Union of European Football Associations, this is the organisation that runs football in Europe.

Yellow card   A card shown by a referee to a cautioned player.

WEBSITES

WWW.FIFA.COM/WORLDCUP/INDEX. HTML

The official webpages for the 2010 World Cup in South Africa, containing links, news and much more.

WWW.PLANETWORLDCUP.COM

A terrific unofficial World Cup website with details of the great players and stories from different tournaments as well as statistics and features.

WWW.WORLDCUP-HISTORY.COM

Learn more about the stats and facts of all World Cups up to and including the 2002 tournament at this website.

WWW.RSSSF.COM/TABLESW/WORLD CUP.HTML

RSSSF is a collection of soccer statisticians and historians and their website may be text only but it is a useful resource with all the games, scorers and details of every World Cup match.

WWW.FIFA.COM/WOMENSWORLDCUP /INDEX.HTML

The official website of the FIFA Women's World Cup with details of past competitions and news of qualifying for the 2011 tournament.

Note to parents and teachers:

Every effort has been made by the publishers to ensure that these websites are suitable for children, that they are of the highest educational value, and that they contain no inappropriate or offensive material. However, because of the nature of the Internet, it is impossible to guarantee that the contents of these sites will not be altered. We strongly advise that Internet access is supervised by a responsible adult.

INDEX